THE COMING OF THE LORD

1 & 2 THESSALONIANS

2 & 3 JOHN

JUDE

STUDIES IN THIS SERIES *Available from your Christian bookstore*

the coming of the Lord

1 & 2 THESSALONIANS

2 & 3 JOHN

JUDE

11 DISCUSSIONS FOR GROUP BIBLE STUDY
MARILYN KUNZ AND CATHERINE SCHELL

TYNDALE HOUSE
PUBLISHERS, INC.
WHEATON, ILLINOIS

Bible verses quoted in this guide are taken from the
New American Standard Bible.

Third printing, December 1986
Library of Congress Catalog Card Number 81-86697
ISBN 0-8423-0424-X
Printed in the United States of America

contents

HOW TO USE THIS DISCUSSION GUIDE

SHARING LEADERSHIP—WHY AND HOW

Each study guide in the Neighborhood Bible Study series is prepared with the intention that the ordinary adult group will by using this guide be able to rotate the leadership of the discussion. Those who are outgoing in personality are more likely to volunteer to lead first, but within a few weeks it should be possible for almost everyone to have the privilege of directing a discussion session. Everyone, including people new to the Bible who may not yet have committed themselves to Christ, should take a turn in leading by asking the questions from the study guide.

Reasons for this approach are:

(1) The discussion leader will prepare in greater depth than the average participant.

(2) The experience of leading a study stimulates a person to be a better participant in the discussions led by others.

(3) Members of the group which changes discussion leadership weekly tend to feel that the group belongs to everyone in it. It is not "Mr. or Mrs. Smith's Bible study."

(4) The Christian who by reason of spiritual maturity and wider knowledge of the Bible is equipped to be a spiritual leader in the group is set free to *listen* to everyone in the group in a way that is not possible when leading the discussion. He (she) takes his regular turn in leading as it comes around,

but if he leads the first study in a series he must guard against the temptation to bring a great deal of outside knowledge and source material which would make others feel they could not possibly attempt to follow his example of leadership.

For study methods and discussion techniques refer to the first booklet in this series, *How to Start a Neighborhood Bible Study,* as well as to the following suggestions.

HOW TO PREPARE TO PARTICIPATE IN A STUDY USING THIS GUIDE

(1) Read through the designated Bible section daily during the week. Use it in your daily time of meditation and prayer, asking God to teach you what he has for you in it.

(2) Take two or three of the guide questions each day and try to answer them from the passage. Use these questions as tools to dig deeper into the passage. In this way you can cover all the guide questions before the group discussion.

(3) Use the summary questions to tie together the whole chapter in your thinking.

(4) *As an alternative* to using this study in your daily quiet time, spend at least an hour in sustained study once during the week, using the above suggestions.

HOW TO PREPARE TO LEAD A STUDY

(1) Follow the above suggestions on preparing to participate in a study. Pray for wisdom and the Holy Spirit's guidance.

(2) Familiarize yourself with the study guide questions until you can rephrase them in your own words if necessary to make you comfortable using them in the discussion.

(3) If you are familiar with the questions in the guide, you will be able to skip questions already answered by the group from discussion raised by another question. Try to get the movement of thought in the whole section for study, so that you are able to be flexible in using the questions.

(4) Pray for the ability to guide the discussion with love and understanding.

HOW TO LEAD A STUDY

(1) Begin with prayer, asking God's help in the study. You may ask another member of the group to pray if you have asked him (her) ahead of time.

(2) Have the Bible portion read aloud by the sections under which questions are grouped in the study guide. It is not necessary for everyone to read aloud, or for each to read an equal amount.

(3) Guide the group to discover what the passage says by asking the *discussion questions.* Use the suggestions from the section on "How to encourage everyone to participate."

(4) *Avoid going rigidly through the study using each and every question.* Be flexible. The group will often answer two or three questions in their discussion of one question. *Omit those questions already answered.* If you cannot discern the meaning of a question, don't use it, or else say to the group that you don't understand the question but they might. If they find it difficult, leave it and try to find the main point of the Bible paragraph.

(5) As the group discusses the Bible passage together, encourage each one to be honest in self-appraisal. If you are honest in your response to the Scripture, others will tend to be honest also.

(6) Allow time at the end of the discussion to answer the summary questions which help to tie the whole study together.

(7) Bring the discussion to a close at the end of the time allotted. Close in prayer, using the prayer written at the end of the study if you wish.

HOW TO ENCOURAGE EVERYONE TO PARTICIPATE

(1) It is helpful to have a number of Bible translations available in the group. Encourage people to read aloud from these different translations as appropriate in the discussion. Many translations have been used in preparation of this study guide.

Particular references have been made to a few by the following abbreviations: JB—Jerusalem Bible; KJV—King James Version; NEB—New English Bible; NIV—New International Version; RSV—Revised Standard Version; TEV—Today's English Version (Good News Bible); TLB—The Living Bible.

(2) Encourage discussion by asking several people to contribute answers to a question. "What do the rest of you think?" or "Is there anything else which could be added?" are ways of encouraging discussion.

(3) Be flexible and skip any questions which do not fit into the discussion as it progresses.

(4) Deal with irrelevant issues by suggesting that the purpose of your study is to discover what is *in the passage.* Suggest an informal chat about tangential or controversial issues after the regular study is dismissed.

(5) Receive all contributions warmly. Never bluntly reject what anyone says, even if you think the answer is incorrect. Instead ask in a friendly manner, "Where did you find that?" or "Is that actually what it says?" or "What do some of the rest of you think?" Allow the group to handle problems together.

(6) Be sure you don't talk too much as the leader. Redirect those questions which are asked you. A discussion should move in the form of an asterisk,

back and forth between members, not in the form of a fan, with the discussion always coming back to the leader. The leader is to act as moderator. As members of a group get to know each other better, the discussion will move more freely, progressing from the fan to the asterisk pattern.

(7) Don't be afraid of pauses or long silences. People need time to think about the questions and the passage. Try *never* to answer your own question —either use an alternate question or move on to another area for discussion.

(8) Watch hesitant members for an indication by facial expression or body posture that they have something to say, and then give them an encouraging nod or speak their names.

(9) Discourage too talkative members from monopolizing the discussion by specifically directing questions to others. If necessary, speak privately to the over-talkative one about the need for discussion rather than lecture in the group, and enlist his aid in encouraging all to participate.

WHAT GUIDELINES MAKE FOR AN EFFECTIVE DISCUSSION?

(1) Everyone in the group should *read the Bible passage* and, if possible, use the study guide in thoughtful *study* of the passage *before* coming to the group meeting.

(2) *Stick to the Bible passage under discussion.* Discover all that you can without moving around to other books of the Bible in cross-references unless such references are suggested in the study guide. The person new to the Bible will not be needlessly confused, and you will avoid the danger of taking portions out of context.

(3) *Avoid tangents.* Many different ideas will come to mind in each study. If a subject is not dealt with in

detail in a particular chapter, do not let it take a lot of your discussion time.

(4) Since the threefold purpose of an inductive Bible study is to discover what the Bible portion says, what it means, and how it may apply in your life, your group should remember that *the Bible is the authority for your study.* The aim of your group should be to discover what Paul or John or Jude is saying in his letter—to discover his message.

(5) If you don't like something that the Bible says, be honest enough to admit that you don't like it. *Do not rewrite the Bible to make it agree with your ideas.* There is a great deal of talk today about the second coming of Christ. The study of the New Testament letters covered in this study guide will give you an opportunity to discover for yourself what Paul and John and Jude had to say about the return of the Lord Jesus Christ.

(6) *Apply to your own life what you discover in this study.* Much of the vitality of any group Bible discussion depends upon honest sharing on the part of different members of the group. The discoveries you make in Bible study should become guides for right attitudes and actions.

(7) *Have an honest and loving attitude in your group toward one another.* Those who have doubts and questions should be able to voice them without feeling rejected by other members of the group. Those who are committed to Jesus Christ as Lord and Savior should be free to share how this belief affects their lives as appropriate to the section under discussion. Rather than seeking to convince one another of your belief or disbelief, you should discover what the Scripture portions have to say to you and face the message of these New Testament letters.

INTRODUCTION TO 1 THESSALONIANS

The existence of this letter testifies to the power of the gospel of Jesus Christ to transform lives. The missionary team of Paul, Silas, and Timothy spent only a few weeks in Thessalonica before some Jews who were jealous of the positive response to Paul's preaching in the synagogue forced them to leave the city.

Thessalonica, capital city of the Roman province of Macedonia, was located on the Egnatian Road which linked Rome with the East. It was the second city to which these missionaries came with the gospel after crossing into what is now called Europe. They came in response to Paul's vision of a man of Macedonia begging him, "Come over to Macedonia and help us" (see Acts 16:6-10).

Their visit probably occurred in the early summer of AD 50, and this first letter to the new church at Thessalonica was written from Corinth during the winter of AD 50-51.

This letter is thought to be the first of Paul's letters to the young churches he founded on his journeys.

DISCUSSION ONE
1 THESSALONIANS 1
TO SERVE THE LIVING AND TRUE GOD,
AND TO WAIT FOR HIS SON FROM HEAVEN

To set the background for understanding Paul's relationship to the people to whom this letter is written, this first discussion will include the study of Acts 17:1-15.

ACTS 17:1-15

1. Locate Amphipolis, Apollonia, and Thessalonica on the map on page 14. How far have Paul and Silas journeyed since they left Syrian Antioch in Acts 15:40?

2. What pattern have Paul and his companions developed as they go to a new town with the gospel message? What is the central theme of Paul's preaching and teaching?

3. What response, positive and negative, is there in Thessalonica?

4. How is the ministry of Paul and his team interrupted? What accusation is made to the city authorities about these missionaries? Compare verse 7 with Luke 23:1, 2. What irony is there in the fact that it is the Jews who bring this accusation?

5. What do Jason and other believers do for Paul? How do you think they feel when Paul and Silas have to leave town at this point?

6. What happier experience do Paul and his companions have at first in Berea? Why? What results from the Bereans' Scripture study? What types of people seem most responsive to Paul's message?

7. How is Paul's ministry again disrupted? What characteristics do you observe in the Thessalonian

Jews who oppose Paul's message? Compare their tactics in verses 5 and 13.

8. If you were Paul, what feelings would you have by this time? Why would Silas and Timothy stay on at Berea for a while?

9. How are people today sometimes divided over the issue of who Jesus is?

1 THESSALONIANS 1:1-10

As you study this letter, keep in mind the events of Acts 17 which attended the beginning of the church at Thessalonica.

10. From verse 1, what do you learn about the senders and the recipients of this letter?

11. What do Paul, Silas (Greek, *Silvanus*), and Timothy especially remember about the Thessalonian Christians as they pray for them?

How and when do you become aware of a person's spiritual life and values? What difference does this make in your relationship with that person?

12. What do *work, labor, perseverance (steadfastness)* suggest to you about the Christian life? Describe situations in which the exercise of faith, or love, or hope is truly demanding work. What is your "work of faith" at this point in your life?

13. Why are the missionaries sure of the reality of the Thessalonians' spiritual experience and faith? Rephrase verses 4, 5a in your own words.

14. Compare Acts 17:5-10a with verse 6. Why do you think that affliction and joy may come together when someone receives the gospel?

15. What pattern is developing in verses 5b-8? What motivated Paul and his co-workers in all they said and did? How did the Thessalonians respond?

16. What have the Thessalonian Christians become

for the other believers on the Grecian peninsula? (Note the location of Macedonia and Achaia on your map on page 14.) What news do Paul and his friends hear of them?

What influence has your faith in God had on others?

17. In verse 8, what two things have become known because of these Christians in Thessalonica? Why are both things needed for the spread of the gospel?

18. What joyous experience do these missionaries describe in verses 8b, 9?

20. If you had only the information in verses 9b, 10, what would you know about the Christian message? Find at least six things. What do you learn about the past, present, and future of these Christians?

Summary

1. Based on the information in Acts 17:1-10, how would you report the events at Thessalonica as a pessimist? As an optimist?

What concerns must Paul have had on being forced to leave the new church just when he felt he was most needed?

2. Based on chapter one of this letter to the Thessalonians, what do you know about what is happening at Thessalonica?

3. What qualities characterize the life of the Thessalonian Christians?

Prayer

O God, all of us are examples to someone of

something. What we look like, what we say, what we do, what we value, what we believe is an example for good or for ill. Whom do I serve? Do I, like the Thessalonian Christians, serve you, the living and true God? Do I wait for your Son from heaven? Lord God, help me to value what you consider important.

DISCUSSION TWO
1 THESSALONIANS 2
BEFORE OUR LORD JESUS AT HIS COMING

In the first chapter Paul, Silas, and Timothy expressed their joy at how the Thessalonian Christians had grown in their faith, and how their faith had influenced and encouraged Christians through Macedonia and Achaia.

1 THESSALONIANS 2:1-8

1. Review the experiences at Philippi to which Paul refers in verse 2. (See Acts 16:11–40.) What had they suffered and why? Consider the possible choices the missionaries faced when they left Philippi.

What do you think motivated them to go on to Thessalonica? At what point would you have been tempted to quit?

2. If you were to use verse 2b as outline for a curriculum to instruct new missionaries, what would you include in the course? See also Romans 1:1-6. What is your definition of *the gospel (Good News) of God*?

3. If verses 3-6 are an answer to accusations against Paul, Silas, and Timothy, what has the opposition been saying? Why is the type of criticism suggested here so difficult to combat?

4. Compare the missionaries' claim to be *approved by God to be entrusted with the gospel* (RSV, NIV) with Paul's experience at his conversion in Acts 9:3-6, 10-16.

5. Contrast the type of leadership which *seeks glory from men* (verse 6) with the leadership described in verses 7, 8. What are the motives and

actions of these contrasting approaches?

Describe your own experience with different types of leaders. What difference has your experience made in the way you want to lead others?

6. Why is the combination of message and concerned messenger (verse 8) so powerful? What difference does it make in your attitudes and behavior if you know that someone genuinely cares for you and desires the best for you?

1 THESSALONIANS 2:9-12

7. Read verse 9 from several translations. How does this verse answer further any accusation that these missionaries' motivation is greed? How is their action here further proof of their love for the Thessalonians?

Note—Paul was a tentmaker by trade, work that could be done anywhere in Macedonia and Achaia. See Acts 18:1-4.

8. Describe the behavior of these communicators of the gospel (verses 10-12). For what it means to *live a life worthy of God* (JB), see also Colossians 1:10-12.

9. If God calls you *into his own kingdom and glory* (RSV), what other kingdoms and glories will you have to forgo? See also Colossians 1:12-14.

10. How do Paul and his companions involve their readers at Thessalonica in thinking about what they are writing them? Trace the phrases that help to accomplish this in verses 1, 9, 10, 11.

1 THESSALONIANS 2:13-16

11. Note the word *also* (verse 13). For what has Paul already thanked God in this letter (1:2, 3)?

For what is he continually thankful? (To recall what the Thessalonians had heard from Paul, see 1:9, 10 and Acts 17:2, 3.)

What have the Thessalonians recognized about this message?

12. How has the experience of the Thessalonian Christians paralleled that of the churches in Judea? With whom else are they identified in their experience of persecution (verse 15)? How would knowing this be an encouragement, do you think?

13. In verses 15, 16, how are all people, particularly the Gentiles (pagans), being opposed or treated as enemies?

What is the serious consequence of standing in the way of another person's spiritual growth? How can we be sure that we are helping, not hindering, another's spiritual life?

14. Summarize the good news and the bad news in this paragraph.

1 THESSALONIANS 2:17-20

15. What mixed feelings of frustration and joy, awareness of time and eternity, and sensitivity to separation and closeness, are expressed in this part of the letter? What is the cause in each case?

16. From this paragraph, what do the Thessalonian Christians surely know about Paul's attitude toward them, and their value to him?

17. What is Paul's expectation concerning what will happen at the coming of our Lord Jesus? How does the awareness of this coming event set the Christian's life and fellowship into perspective?

Summary

1. List all the characteristics of Paul and his

fellow missionaries from what is said and the way it is said in this chapter. Which are the most important to you, and why?

2. What clues do you find that indicate that Paul and the others worked with individuals as well as with the Thessalonian Christians as a group?

Prayer

Dear Lord, how much suffering and humiliation, how much opposition, inconvenience, and embarrassment am I willing to endure in order to communicate the gospel to another person? How much time and effort, how much of myself, am I prepared to invest to have such hope and joy as this letter speaks of before you, Lord Jesus, at your coming?

In the letter thus far, Paul, Silas, and Timothy have reviewed the nature of their ministry in Thessalonica, their motives, their methods, and their message. Paul congratulates the Thessalonian Christians for their faith, acknowledging the suffering they have had to endure. He expresses his deep longing to see them.

1 THESSALONIANS 3:1-5

1. How does Paul explain his actions in sending Timothy back to Thessalonica? What could Paul bear no longer?

2. How is Timothy described? What does this description suggest about the appropriate relationship between Christians? Why is Timothy not Paul's servant?

What is one called to do as God's servant in the gospel of Christ? See also Matthew 28:19, 20.

3. What are the two parts of Timothy's mission as described in verses 2b, 3? How had Paul already prepared these Christians for possible afflictions and trials? See also Acts 14:21, 22 for what Paul had learned and taught on his first missionary journey.

4. Compare Paul's concern for the Thessalonians with the parable Jesus explained in Mark 4:14-20. In Jesus' parable what types of afflictions destroyed the faith of those who had received the word?

5. How had Paul prepared the Thessalonians (verse 4)? See also 2:11, 12. Describe how you would try to prepare someone to face situations which could be detrimental to his or her faith. What values and what

perspective would you be concerned to share? Why?

6. What insight do you get into the level of Paul's concern, from verse 5? What did he have to sacrifice to get the information he wanted? How do you imagine that Timothy conveyed Paul's concern when he arrived back at Thessalonica? How does it help you when you realize that others are concerned for your spiritual wellbeing?

7. How does Paul express the nature of his fears? Describe similar concerns you may have had for others. Compare verse 5b with 2:18, and with Mark 4:15.

1 THESSALONIANS 3:6-10

8. What change of mood occurs between verses 5 and 6? Why? What specific things does Timothy report? What indication is there that Paul has other problems at the time of writing this letter?

9. Do you think that Paul's vulnerability was a part of his strength, or a sign of weakness? Explain.

10. What specifically did Timothy report concerning the Thessalonians? How do Paul and his companions indicate that their own welfare is closely linked to that of the Thessalonian Christians? What effect will the Thessalonians' continued steadfastness have upon Paul and Silas and Timothy?

11. In verse 9, what happy dilemma do the writers face? It is said that one can learn a great deal about a person's value system by observing what makes him happy or sad. What do you learn about Paul and his companions by such observations? What would someone learn about you by noting what makes you happy?

12. What new prayer does Paul pray now that he has been assured of the Thessalonians' love for him? Why

is there much these Christians have yet to learn (verse 10)?

Note—Paul and Silas had been able to stay only a few weeks in Thessalonica before their forced departure. The bond Jason and his fellow Christians had to post with the city officials apparently prevented Paul and Silas' return.

1 THESSALONIANS 3:11-13

13. What are the three requests of this prayer? What does the first request reveal about Paul's understanding of the relationship between the Lord Jesus and God the Father?

14. What connection is indicated between a Christian's relationship to fellow Christians and other people, and to God (verses 12, 13)? What example have the Thessalonians had in Paul, Silas, and Timothy?

15. What ultimate goal does Paul pray for the Thessalonian Christians? See also 1 Corinthians 1:7, 8.

16. Compare verse 13 with 1:10. With what expectation does Paul carry on his missionary activities? To what extent do you think Christians today live and work in anticipation of *the coming of our Lord Jesus with all his saints?* How would this affect one's perspective?

Note—*Saints* may also be translated *holy ones*, and may refer to angelic hosts attending Jesus' return, or to believers who have already died.

Summary

1. Some people think of the Apostle Paul only as the architect of Christian theology. What sort of

person with what range of emotions does this chapter reveal him to be?

2. Trace the expression *your faith* in verses 2, 5, 7, 10. What concerns Paul and Silas, and Timothy in this chapter? How do you express similar concerns for others? Give examples.

Prayer

Lord Jesus Christ, help me to learn appropriate concerns for others and for myself. Let my thoughts and emotions, my values and my energies be devoted to the things that you value. Help me to keep the perspective which sets all time into your hands, remembering that you will come again.

With Timothy's return from a visit to Thessalonica (chapter 3), Paul has been assured of the faith of the Thessalonian Christians and of their affection for him. While Paul hopes to get back to Thessalonica eventually to instruct them further in the faith, he takes this section of the letter to highlight certain aspects of the Christian life he wants them to remember.

Paul must have been painfully aware that his short stay in Thessalonica could scarcely have been enough to leave there a firmly grounded Christian church.

1 THESSALONIANS 4:1-8

1. What evidences do you observe of Paul as parent, coach, and teacher in verses 1, 2? What weight do the phrases *in the Lord Jesus* and *through (by the authority of) the Lord Jesus* give to Paul's teaching?

2. From verse 1 what was the aim of the teachings Paul and his companions gave the Thessalonians while they were with them? To what extent does this aim guide and govern the decisions you make in your daily life?

3. How might you use verse 3a to counsel the young person who keeps asking, "How can I know the will of God for my life?" See also Romans 12:1, 2.

4. Read verses 3–8 in at least three translations. From these verses list what God wants (what is the will of God) for each of us.

Note—Verse 4—the Greek word for *vessel* used here is translated *body* in 5:23, and is more appropriately translated *his own body* (NIV) or *the body that belongs to him* (JB) rather than *wife.*

5. What indicates clearly to Paul that the heathen (pagans) do not know God? How do you think Paul would view your community in this regard? Why?

Of what previous warning does Paul remind the Thessalonians?

6. To what (verse 7) is a Christian called? Compare with 1 Peter 2:9, 10.

7. How is the seriousness of what is said emphasized in each verse in verses 6-8?

8. What connection do you see between the Spirit which God gives to Christians and the kind of life God calls us to live?

1 THESSALONIANS 4:9-12

9. After complimenting the Thessalonians on their love of their fellow Christians, what three exhortations does Paul give them? What danger is implied in verse 12?

How might their concern over the imminence of the Lord's return cause the members of the young church to act in ways that would lose the respect of the society around them and eventually cause financial problems.?

1 THESSALONIANS 4:13-18

10. What apparently has Timothy reported to Paul about what is troubling the Thessalonian Christians? Why are they particularly grieved about those in their group who have died?

11. Of what does Paul assure them about these deceased believers? What is the reason for his strong assurance?

12. List the sequence of events described in verses 16, 17. Compare Acts 1:11.

Note—*To meet the Lord,* verse 17: In the Greek-speaking world of Paul's day, when a king paid an official visit to a city, leading citizens and chief officials of the city would go out to meet him and escort him on the final part of his journey into the city.

What does this add to your understanding of the events Paul describes?

13. What does Paul set in contrast to the grieving without hope of verse 13? What are Christians to do with this knowledge? How does all of this make Christianity unique?

14. What does the statement *and so we shall always be with the Lord* (verse 17b, RSV) mean to you? What do you imagine were Paul's emotions as he wrote this?

Note—For further information about the return of Christ and the resurrection of believers in Christ, read 1 Corinthians 15, and 2 Corinthians 5:1-10. Paul also handles the subject further in his second letter to the Thessalonians.

Summary

1. With what major teachings and events is Paul concerned in this chapter? What phrases does he use to encourage the Thessalonian believers to go on in their life in Christ?

2. How does Paul clarify a particular area of concern which is troubling these Christians?

Prayer

Dear Lord, I really like those Christians at Thessalonica. They seem so eager to please you. It's easy to understand why Paul was so fond of them. Help me to be more like them in my desire to understand your will and to do it.

In the earlier parts of this letter, the Thessalonian Christians have been encouraged to continue in the way Paul and his companions had instructed them when they were with them. They are reminded not to follow the loose sexual ways of those who do not know God. They are to work diligently and to continue to love one another.

In response to their concern that Christians who have died will not participate in the Lord's triumphant return, Paul has informed the Thessalonians that believers who have died will rise to life first to join those still living, who are gathered up to meet their returning Lord in the air.

1 THESSALONIANS 5:1-11

1. Read 4:16—5:11. In which section does Paul seem to give new information, and in which does he review what he has previously communicated?

Note—Verse 2, *day of the Lord,*—is an Old Testament term referring to God's future intervention in history both in salvation and judgment. In the New Testament, it is a comprehensive term designating all the events involved in the second coming of Christ. See also 2 Peter 3:10.

2. Compare 5:2 with Matthew 24:42-44. How is the idea of the unexpectedness of the expected event illustrated in verse 3? How does this illustration emphasize the impossibility of escaping the events of *the day of the Lord?* Upon whom will destruction come? Note the *but* in verse 4.

3. What two different groups of people are

described in verses 3–8? List their characteristics.

4. How are Christians to live until Christ returns (verses 6–8, 11)?

5. Compare verse 8 with Ephesians 6:13–17. What purposes do the *breastplate* and the *helmet* serve in the soldier's armor? In the spiritual armor of the Christian?

6. In what three different ways is *sleep (asleep)* used in verses 6, 7, 10?

7. Concerning God's wrath, compare verse 9; 1:10; and Romans 5:9, 10.

Note—God's wrath is his permanent and consistent attitude, as a holy and just God, toward sin and evil. Until the final day of wrath, God's wrath is always tempered with mercy, especially in his dealings with his chosen people. Jesus experienced on our behalf and in our place the afflictions, punishment, and death which belong to sinners subject to God's wrath.

8. From verses 9, 10, what are the results, for believers, of Christ's death?

9. What does Paul urge the Thessalonian Christians to do because of all he has told them?

1 THESSALONIANS 5:12-22

10. What specific instructions does this section give Christians to help them to please God (4:1) and to encourage one another in spiritual growth (5:11)?

11. From these verses what do you learn about the early structure of the church at Thessalonica?

Note—See Acts 14:21–23 for Paul's practice of appointing *elders* in the churches he founded on his missionary journeys.

12. From this section what clues do you observe about the temptations faced by the Thessalonian Christians? Which of these do you meet today? Which

do you find most difficult to handle and why?

With verse 15 see Jesus' teaching in Matthew 5:43-45, and Paul's later teaching in Ephesians 4:32.

13. Review the circumstances (Acts 16:22-25) which Paul and Silas had faced immediately before their visit to Thessalonica. How have they earned the right to be taken seriously in the commands they give in verses 16-18?

14. What balance do the commands of verses 19-22 suggest for the worship activities of the church at Thessalonica?

15. What is the danger when a church or an individual fails to *test everything?* What standards have the Thessalonians been given against which any "message from God" should be tested? Note 3:12—4:12; 5:8, 11.

1 THESSALONIANS 5:23-28

16. Read verses 23, 24 in at least three translations. Rephrase these verses in your own words.

17. What do you learn about God in verses 23, 24? What will God do for those whom he *calls* (4:7; 5:24)? Compare verse 23 and 3:13.

18. How does this prayer summarize what the missionaries want for the young Christians to whom this letter is written?

19. Put into your own words the message of each of the last four verses of this letter. What does this closing add to your understanding of the relationship Paul and his companions have with this young church?

Summary

1. What is the Christian's way of life to be?
2. What is the Christian's final destiny?

Overview of 1 Thessalonians:

1. From what perspective do Paul and his companions see the Christian life? How is this viewpoint to affect the way the Thessalonians live?
See: 1 Thessalonians 1:9, 10
2:19
3:12, 13
4:13, 16–18
5:2, 9–11

2. What place does this emphasis have in your thinking?

Prayer

Lord Jesus Christ, it is hard to keep a proper balance in our thinking about your return in power. If we focus only on your return, we can become careless about our responsibilities to our generation. We may even fail to share the good news of your salvation. If we ignore your coming return, we can fall into the trap of thinking that this world is all there is, that evil is unconquerable, and that holy lives do not matter.

INTRODUCTION TO 2 THESSALONIANS

Although scholars argue various possibilities about the timing and authorship of this letter, it is generally concluded that this second letter to the church at Thessalonica was written from Corinth by Paul, with Silas and Timothy, not long after the first letter.

Apparently further news of the Thessalonians had reached Paul, and this letter was to clarify his teaching about the Lord's return. The Thessalonian Christians seem so impressed by the suddenness of the second coming (1 Thess. 5:2, 3) that they believe it may occur immediately. They still seem to be speculating about the expected return of the Lord to the detriment of the present quality of their Christian life.

The Thessalonians are an example of what happens when a church or an individual becomes unbalanced spiritually by focusing on one truth to such an extent that the result is untruthful. Paul hastens to address the problem, trying to put some of the Thessalonians' concerns into proper perspective and to refocus their attention on their immediate responsibilities, as well as on the future victory of Christ in his coming in glory.

In reading the letters to the Thessalonians, we don't know precisely what information Paul, Silas, and Timothy received from, and about, the church at Thessalonica between the two letters. We can only observe this second letter for clues.

2 THESSALONIANS 1:1, 2

1. Compare the salutation here with that in 1 Thessalonians. How is the group of Christians to whom these letters are written identified?

Note—*Grace*, the greeting with which Greek letters always began; *peace*, the normal greeting with which one Jew met another.

2 THESSALONIANS 1:3, 4

2. Read these verses in several translations. How would you feel if you received this message? Of what two things do the writers take note (verse 3)? See also James 2:14–17. How are the Thessalonians meeting the test of faith?

3. What do you understand from verse 4 about what has been happening in Thessalonica? What are the missionaries telling other churches about the Thessalonian Christians? Review some of the accusations these Christians may be facing (Acts 17:6–9).

4. Give examples of Christians today suffering persecution and afflictions for their faith.

2 THESSALONIANS 1:5-12

5. For what are the Thessalonian Christians

suffering? What do their attitudes and actions prove?

Compare verses 5, 11a, and 1 Thessalonians 2:12. Of what are they *worthy?* What does it mean to be *worthy?*

6. Discuss the possible ways the Thessalonians could view their sufferings. Review briefly Jesus' teaching about the characteristics of those who are part of the kingdom of God (Matt. 5:3-12).

7. As this letter moves from the present (verse 5) to the future (verses 6-10), what effect do you think this letter might have on its first readers?

8. How are the people characterized who are afflicting the Christians in Thessalonica (verse 8)? What will happen to these persecutors, and when? Note the two major aspects of their punishment (verse 9).

9. How would you paint the picture described in verses 7b-10?

10. In what way is the future as seen in verses 8, 9 simply an extension of the present described in verse 8?

11. Review the message Paul preached in Thessalonica and the reactions to it (Acts 17:2-5). What decision has been made by those who are troubling the Thessalonian Christians?

12. What does it mean to *not obey the gospel of our Lord Jesus Christ* (verse 8)? How is obeying the gospel of the Lord Jesus related to knowing God? See also John 17:1-3.

13. Why is simply hearing the message of Christ not enough? Review the warning Jesus gave in a parable in Matthew 7:24-27.

What had some in Thessalonica heard but refused to accept and act upon in faith? Where may such people be found today?

14. What contrast is drawn in verses 9, 10? How does Paul draw his readers into the picture in verse 10?

15. What are the five parts of Paul's prayer in verses 11, 12? What would you answer if someone were to ask you, "What are your desires for goodness today?" or "How are you putting your faith to work?"

16. How is the name of Jesus honored because of virtues evident in the lives of Christians you know?

Summary

How would this chapter meet the needs of Christians who are suffering persecution because of their faith in Jesus Christ?

Prayer

Lord Jesus, my faith needs to grow, to be stretched and exercised. My love for other Christians must increase. By your own power, fulfill all my desire for goodness, and complete my work of faith. May your name be more highly thought of because of the way I live by your power and your grace.

In the first chapter Paul has told the Thessalonians he is aware of what has been happening to them. He commends them for their continued faith under fire. He assures them that those who trouble them will ultimately suffer eternal destruction, while they will enjoy the presence of the Lord and participate in his glory.

In this chapter Paul comes to his main reason for writing them so soon after his first letter. Scholars point out that this is one of the most difficult passages in the New Testament. Part of the problem is that Paul bases what he writes here on verbal teaching he gave while in Thessalonica, teaching to which we have no access, thus making much of this chapter obscure.

2 THESSALONIANS 2:1–12

1. Read verses 1, 2 from several different translations, including TEV. What has upset the young Christians in Thessalonica? What are the three avenues of incorrect information? Why would the last be particularly unsettling?

2. Read 1 Thessalonians 4:13–18. *The day of the Lord* includes many events. The report that these events have begun to take place (*the day of the Lord has come,* verse 2) would lead people to expect that the coming of the Lord himself and the gathering of believers to him would certainly occur shortly.

Whatever report they have heard, what does Paul make very clear in verses 3, 4?

3. What things must take place before the coming

of the Lord? What ideas are suggested by the words *rebellion, lawlessness, opposes, exalts?*

4. In what particular area does this man make his claims? To what degree does he exalt himself?

5. What do the Thessalonian Christians seem to have forgotten? List what Paul reviews for them in verses 6–8.

6. Why is this *lawless one* not ultimately to be feared? How will he be destroyed?

7. In relation to the concept of lawlessness in verses 7–9, see the *law* in Matthew 22:36–40.

8. Who is behind the activities of the *man of lawlessness* (NIV, RSV), the *man of rebellion* (TLB), *the Wicked One* (TEV)? What sort of things will accompany his coming (verses 9, 10)?

9. Why should pretense and deception be expected? What was the first deception in Genesis 3?

10. Compare verses 9, 10 with Jesus' warning in Mark 13:22. Why should people not be swayed by *signs and wonders?* What tragic examples can you think of in which people have been swayed by false messiahs and false teachers? How may this happen even within a local church?

11. Read verses 9–12 in several translations. Compare with Romans 1:18–25. In both references, what precedes God's action?

12. List all the contrasts in verses 6–12. How do you see these contrasts operating in the lives of men and women today?

13. What truth must be believed? See 1 Thessalonians 1:9, 10; 2:13. What tends to be characteristic of those who reject the truth?

2 THESSALONIANS 2:13-15

14. What change of mood do you see in this paragraph in contrast to the previous section? On

what does Paul now focus his attention?

How does he address his readers? Why does he consider himself obligated to thank God for them?

15. Compare verse 13b with 1 Thessalonians 1:4 and Ephesians 1:4. What is God's activity for their salvation? What is theirs? Compare with the response of those in verse 10b. What definition of salvation can you give from verse 13?

16. What does it mean to you to *believe in the truth?*

17. Compare Romans 8:14–17 and John 17:20–23 with verse 14. Since the Christians at Thessalonica are going through affliction and persecution, what perspective will verses 13, 14 give them? How will this help them to endure?

18. What are the two parts of Paul's exhortation in verse 15? What kind of situation has Paul been trying to prepare them for in verses 3–5? What have they already experienced (1:4)?

What tests do Christians (whom you know) face today? How are you preparing to face tests to your faith?

2 THESSALONIANS 2:16, 17

19. What is Paul's twofold prayer for these Christians whom he dearly loves? Why do you think he is confident that his prayer for them will be answered?

Note—The word *comfort* means to strengthen, as preparing for battle.

Summary

1. How did the Thessalonians react to the rumor that the day of the Lord had already come? What does Paul say to clarify the matter for them?

2. How does he reassure them regarding their spiritual status? What does he want them to do?

Prayer

Lord, help me to trust you about those things in this chapter that I don't fully understand, and to concentrate on the things from this chapter which are clear. Help me to stand firm in my faith in the gospel and not to be shaken by spiritual enemies of the gospel. Deepen my understanding of your Word, and strengthen my commitment to you, Lord Jesus Christ.

In the previous chapter Paul described a great impostor who will claim to be God, and with whom the Lord Jesus will do battle at his coming. Those who have refused the truth of the gospel will believe instead the lie of the impostor. Paul has appealed to these young believers to stand firm and hold to the teachings he and Silas and Timothy have given them in person or by letter.

2 THESSALONIANS 3:1-5

1. Chapter 2 closed with a prayer for the Thessalonians. Now what two things does Paul ask them to pray for him and his companions?

What insight do these requests give you into Paul's goals and the circumstances in which he works? What is his first concern?

2. What two experiences regarding faith does Paul comment on in verses 2b, 3a? In dire circumstances what may Christians rely upon?

What two things will the Lord do for the Christian? See also Matthew 6:13 and John 17:15.

3. What balance in the Christian's life is suggested by what the Lord does and what the Christian does (verses 3, 4)? What are some of the commmands Paul has given them? See 1 Thessalonians 4:2-7, 10-12; 5:12-22.

4. How do you respond when someone speaks to you in the way that Paul does to the Thessalonians in verse 4? Why?

5. Discuss verse 5, taking it in two different ways: first, that the prayer is for the Thessalonians to be

appreciative recipients of these graces; and second, that they are to exhibit these characteristics as Christians.

2 THESSALONIANS 3:6-13

6. Read verse 4 and follow immediately with verses 6-13. What strong action do the missionaries call for? Why? Compare with 1 Thessalonians 5:14. On what authority do they give the order?

7. Compare the way in which the missionaries speak in verse 6 with the way an ambassador delivers messages on behalf of his sovereign. Why do they not speak in their own name?

8. What example have the missionaries themselves given by the things they did and did not do while they were in Thessalonica? What were their reasons for this behavior?

9. How is a Christian community or church burdened if some live in idleness? How have you been influenced, positively or negatively, by the actions of spiritual leaders?

10. What simple operating principle did the missionaries give the church when they were in Thessalonica (verse 10)?

11. What two life styles are contrasted in verses 11, 12? To what unfortunate pastime does idleness lead?

12. Compare the admonition in verse 13 with Galatians 6:9, 10. Under what circumstances are you tempted to become *weary of doing good (tire of doing what is right,* NIV)? Why?

2 THESSALONIANS 3:14-18

13. How is the command in verse 6 reinforced in verses 14, 15? What goal is stated? What hope is implied?

14. What attitude is to control the way in which these commands are carried out?

15. What is the emphasis of the closing prayer (verse 16)? Compare with Jesus' promises in John 14:27 and 16:33.

16. If Jesus is the Lord of peace, at what times and in what ways can he give you peace where now you do not have it?

17. What possible reasons can you think of for Paul to make his handwriting familiar to the Thessalonians? See 2:2, 3a.

What final benediction does he add to the *peace* in verse 16? What is the source of peace and grace for the Christian?

Summary

Have this chapter read aloud from a contemporary translation by one individual. Everyone in the group should play the part of a Christian at Thessalonica hearing this letter read for the first time, sensitive to each emotion and idea expressed.

How do you feel about this chapter? What ideas impressed you?

Discuss what you think you ought to do about this portion of the letter. What attitudes do you have? What actions will you take?

Prayer

God our Father, there is a lot of talk about "burn out" these days, even among Christians. In evil times there is great temptation to become weary of doing what is right. Lead us into a greater understanding of your love, and the endurance you give. Give us your peace at all times. Strengthen us to serve you and to communicate your message to our generation. Increase the ranks of your faithful servants. In Jesus' name. Amen.

INTRODUCTION TO 2 JOHN AND 3 JOHN

These two letters are distinguished not only by their brevity but also by the fact that they may be dated among the last of the New Testament books. There has been some disagreement among scholars over the years concerning the authorship of these letters, but there is no external evidence to dispute the traditional view that the author of 2 and 3 John is the same as the author of 1 John, the Apostle John, the son of Zebedee.

The books of 2 and 3 John deal with the theme of hospitality, particularly showing hospitality to traveling teachers in the early church.

The Book of 3 John is clearly addressed to an individual, but there is some dispute as to whether 2 John is addressed to an individual and her family on whether the form of address is a symbolic way of writing to a church. In either case, both letters are clearly concerned with the problems arising from the fact that a number of teachers are traveling around to the churches, receiving hospitality in the homes of leading Christians.

2 JOHN 1-3

1. Read these verses from several translations. To whom is the letter addressed? How does the author identify himself? What is the basis of the affection he expresses? For whom does he speak besides himself?

2. Trace each reference to *truth* in verses 1-3. What difference does *the truth* make? Compare with references to the truth in 1 John 1:5-10. What truth lives or abides in Christians? (See verse 2 and 1 John 1:8, 9; 5:20.)

3. Look up *grace, mercy,* and *peace* in the dictionary. Discuss the definitions which you think apply to this benediction.

2 JOHN 4-11

4. What has made the writer happy? What truth is he apparently referring to? Trace the reference to *commanded* and *commandments* in verses 4-6. What is the writer's circular reasoning concerning love and commandments?

5. What does the writer call upon people to do? What do the phrases *follow* (RSV), *walk in* (KJV), *live in* (NIV, TEV) add to your understanding of this call to love and to obey? What does it mean to you to *walk in love* and to *walk in obedience* (verse 6)?

6. How has the emphasis on *the truth* at the beginning of the letter prepared readers for the warning in verses 7 and following? What is happening in the church of that day?

7. Compare verse 7 with 1 John 2:22–25; 4:1–3. Why is a refusal to acknowledge the incarnation essentially a rejection of the Christian faith? See also Philippians 2:5–11.

8. What great danger is pointed out in verses 8, 9? What "advanced" or "progressive" teaching did John warn against?

Note—This warning was in line with the attempt being made by some in the early church to bring gnostic teachings into Christianity, particularly the idea that all matter is evil.

9. How is the doctrine that Jesus Christ came in the flesh as a human being to be used as a test (verse 10)? what action is necessary toward teachers who do not hold to the proper doctrine, the reality of the incarnation? Why is it necessary to be so inhospitable?

2 JOHN 12, 13

10. Why doesn't the author continue, though he has much more to write?

11. In our day of many cults, what truths about Jesus Christ in verses 3 and 7 are the standard by which you can test the ideas of religious teachers, books, and organizations?

3 JOHN 1-8

12. Read through the letter, observing the repetition and use of the word *truth,* which also concerned the writer in the previous letter.

13. What has the writer recently heard about Gaius? From whom? How does he react to such information? What does this reveal about the writer's values?

What kinds of things bring you joy? Why?

14. For what does the writer commend Gaius? Contrast verse 6b with his instructions in 2 John 10, 11.

15. What further information do you learn about the brethren? Why should such people be supported by their fellow Christians?

How does it affect the amount you give to those who teach and preach the gospel when you remember that such giving makes you a *fellow worker in the truth?*

3 JOHN 9-12

16. List five or six things you learn here about Diotrephes. What do his actions reveal about him (verse 11)? What sort of things would Diotrephes do in a local church today?

17. What clear advice does the writer give Gaius? Why should he not be influenced by a person like Diotrephes? What actions does he imply he wants Gaius to take on behalf of Demetrius in spite of Diotrephes' presence in the church?

3 JOHN 13, 14

18. Compare verses 13, 14 with 2 John 12. Why is *peace* an appropriate benediction for Gaius, who must meet the situations mentioned in this letter?

Summary

1. What warnings do these two brief letters give against deceivers?

2. What examples do these letters give of those who follow the truth?

Prayer

Lord, help me to be a follower of truth. Strengthen me to stand against those who would deceive me and deceive others. Help me to be one in whom others see the way to truth. In your name, the name of Jesus who is the way, the truth, and the life. Amen.

INTRODUCTION TO JUDE

The letter of Jude belongs to that group of New Testament letters which are not addressed to particular persons or to a local church. The other letters in this category are James, 1 and 2 Peter, and 1 John.

Scholars point out the similarity between 2 Peter and Jude, and there is debate as to which writer quoted the other, or whether both referred to a third source.

Scholars believe that the author Jude is best identified as the brother of Jesus in Matthew 13:55: "Is not this the carpenter's son? Is not His mother called Mary, and His brothers, James and Joseph and Simon and Judas [Jude]?" His brother James (Jude, verse 1) was the leader of the church in Jerusalem and presided over the Council in Jerusalem described in Acts 15. It was to James that Paul and the other missionaries reported when they returned to Jerusalem from their journey in Acts 21:18.

DISCUSSION TEN
JUDE 1-13
CONTEND FOR THE FAITH

Although Jude's original intention was to write a treatise on the Christian faith, he apparently had to forgo this longer work to deal with what he considers a clear and present danger to the church. William Barclay comments about his letter, "There have indeed been times in the history of the Church, and especially in the revivals of the Church, when Jude was not far off from being the most relevant book in the New Testament."

JUDE 1, 2

1. By what relationships does Jude identify himself for his readers? What does this reveal about Jude? Compare with James 1:1; Galatians 1:19.

2. Read these verses in NEB, NIV, RSV, TEV, and TLB. By what three phrases does Jude describe those to whom he is writing?

What does each of these truths mean in your life?

JUDE 3, 4

3. How does this letter differ in style and content from the one which Jude had planned to write? What does he want the readers of this letter to do?

4. What does the phrase *once for all,* or *once and for all,* tell you about *the faith* delivered to the saints (entrusted to God's people)?

5. Read verses 3, 4 in several translations. What is the source of the immediate danger to which Jude directs his readers' attention?

6. How does Jude describe certain people who

have *secretly slipped in* (NIV) among the Christians to whom he writes? By what actions and by what teachings do these people undermine the faith?

7. These infiltrators into the church are distorting the message about the grace of God, turning it into an excuse for immorality. Contrast this with the Apostle Paul's reasoning in his letter to the Romans (6:1, 2, 15–18).

8. How are the uniqueness of Jesus Christ, his incarnation and deity, under attack in our day?

In what ways is *our only Master and Lord, Jesus Christ*, disowned and immorality made acceptable in the church today?

JUDE 5-7

9. Of what three events does Jude remind his readers? What was the sin in each case? The result? What does Jude want his readers to learn from history?

Note—If you are not familiar with the Old Testament events to which verses 5 and 7 refer, you may wish to read in your study preparation: Genesis 18:20, 21; 19:1–29; Exodus 12:29–42, 51; Numbers 13:1, 2, 25–33; 14:1–38.

10. What can happen to those who have experienced the Lord's blessing and deliverance (verse 5)? Why?

11. In what way did some of the angelic beings rebel? What is their present state?

Note—Verse 6 may allude to the incident in Genesis 6:1–4, an incident described more elaborately in Jewish apocryphal writings to which Jude refers later in the letter.

12. Of what are Sodom and Gomorrah to serve as a warning?

13. In spite of the examples just cited, what three things are the people (about whom Jude has warned them in verse 4) doing in verse 8?

14. How does verse 9 illustrate the seriousness of their action in being contemptuous of angels *(glorious ones,* RSV, *celestial beings, NEB)*? What did even the archangel Michael not presume to do? In contrast, what do these men do in verse 10a?

15. Read verse 10 in several translations. How are the actions described of these people who are infecting the church?

16. With what three Old Testament persons does Jude compare these people?

17. What did Cain do and why? (See Genesis 4:1-16.)

18. Balaam (Numbers 22:1—25:9; 31:7-16) is noted for his greed and for leading Israel into Baal worship. (See Revelation 2:14.)

Korah (Numbers 16) rebelled against Moses, God's chosen leader for Israel.

What insight do these illustrations give you into what is going on in the church (or churches) to which Jude writes?

19. What do you learn about these false teachers in Jude's description in verse 12a? What effects would such attitudes and behavior have on the fellowship of the church?

Note—Verse 12a, *love feasts:* in the early church this was an evening meal accompanied or followed by celebration of the Lord's Supper (Eucharist).

20. Read verses 12, 13 in several translations. What five vivid metaphors does Jude use to describe these dangerous people? What do you learn about them from each picture?

Summary

This will be included with the next discussion.

Prayer

Lord, as Christians in today's world, we do not often think about the need to guard against evil from within the church. Yet if anything is destroying the church today it is the very things Jude mentions: unbelief, immorality, jealousy, greed, pride, and power. Help us to strive against these things within ourselves and within the church.

In the first part of his letter Jude calls upon his readers to contend for the faith against ungodly people who have slipped into the church. He cites God's judgments against unbelieving Israelites who did not enter the promised land, rebellious angels, and the immoral people of Sodom and Gomorrah. Jude warns his readers that these people are repeating the murderous jealousy of Cain, the greed of Balaam which led to immorality in Israel, and Korah's attitude of rebellion against God's leaders. If they are not dealt with, they carry the seeds of destruction for the church.

JUDE 14-16

1. What point does Jude make by his quotation from Enoch? What is the effect of his repetition of *all* and of *ungodly* (RSV, NIV)?

Note—The book of Enoch is a writing not included in the Jewish list of accepted Scriptures but one that Jude assumes is familiar to, and respected by, his readers.

2. What particular sins of speech does Jude add (verse 16) in his continuing description of those he indicts? What motivates these people?

JUDE 17-23

3. Note the change of tone introduced here by the words, *but you . . . beloved (dear friends)*, in verses 17, 20.

4. Of what prediction by the apostles does Jude

remind his readers? Compare 2 Peter 3:3, 4. What is the motivating drive of these scoffers (verses 18, 19)? What effect do they have on the church?

5. How do you act in the presence of those who are scornful of the Christian faith? How do you feel if such scorn is directed at you because you are a Christian?

6. Read verse 19 in several translations. What three things characterize these people?

7. In contrast, what four things (verses 20, 21) should Christians do? Note the references in these verses to the different persons of the Trinity.

8. Read verses 22, 23 in at least three translations. In addition to nourishing and developing his own spiritual life, what responsibility is the Christian to show toward others? What actions should one take, what attitudes is one to have, toward those who begin to follow these false teachers, perhaps even toward the false teachers themselves?

JUDE 24, 25

9. About what two things is Jude confident? How is the one described to whom this prayer of praise is addressed?

10. What four qualities are ascribed to God? For how long is this true of God?

Summary

1. If you had been in the group that received Jude's letter, how would both its salutation and its ending help you to act on the warnings he gives in the body of the letter?

2. What are the basic sins of the people about whom Jude warns his readers? Unless those people

repent, what is in store for them? In contrast, what awaits God's people?

Review of 1 and 2 Thessalonians, 2 and 3 John, Jude

Even a superficial reading of these letters makes it clear that the writers—Paul, Silas, Timothy; John; Jude—looked at their times in light of the expected return of the Lord Jesus Christ in power.

Christians keep their balance in unsettling times and difficult situations with the certain hope that ultimately all things will come under the gloriously revealed power and authority of the One whom they love and serve.

1. This guide is subtitled "The Coming of the Lord." Review each letter, reading aloud the title for each discussion and the following verses, commenting on the impact of each reference as you go along:

1 Thessalonians 1:9, 10
2:19, 20
3:11–13
4:16–18
5:1–4

2 Thessalonians 1:5–12
2:8
3:3

2 John 7
3 John 3, 4
Jude 21, 24, 25

Like each major doctrine of the Christian faith, the doctrine of the second coming of Christ has had periods of neglect and periods of overemphasis in the history of the church. Paul deals with such neglect and overemphasis in 1 and 2 Thessalonians.

In any period, however, the Christian's world and life view must be tempered by remembering that an end is coming to the world as we know it, a time when God will intervene in power to bring every knee to bow and every tongue to confess that Jesus Christ is Lord. (See Philippians 2:8–11.)

2. What new knowledge have you gained about the return of Jesus Christ?

3. What practical difference will this knowledge make in your life this year?

Prayer

Read Psalm 121, followed by Jude 24, 25 as your closing prayer.